ANIMALS that LAY EGGS

**Created by
Peter M. Spizzirri**

This Is An Educational FACTS AND FUN Book of ANIMALS THAT LAY EGGS • Published by SPIZZIRRI PUBLISHING, INC., P.O. BOX 9397, RAPID CITY, SOUTH DAKOTA 57709.
Printed in U.S.A.

EMU

Dromaius novaehollandiae

The male emu is a wonderful father. He helps build a nest of twigs and leaves. After the female lays the eggs, he takes over the incubation (hatching) of them. He seldom eats and doesn't drink for 8 weeks until the chicks are hatched.

••

The Australian emu averages 12 eggs a season, each weighing 1 to 1 1/2 pounds.

EMU

Dromaius novaehollandiae

CHINOOK SALMON

Oncorhynchus tshawytscha

Chinook salmon live in the ocean but are born in fresh water streams. Salmon fight their way upstream (against currents and up rapids) to spawn in the same stream where they were born. Salmon can grow to be 58 inches long and weigh up to 126 pounds.

A Chinook of the Yukon River will travel over 2000 miles to lay up to 5000 eggs.

CHINOOK SALMON

Oncorhynchus tshawytscha

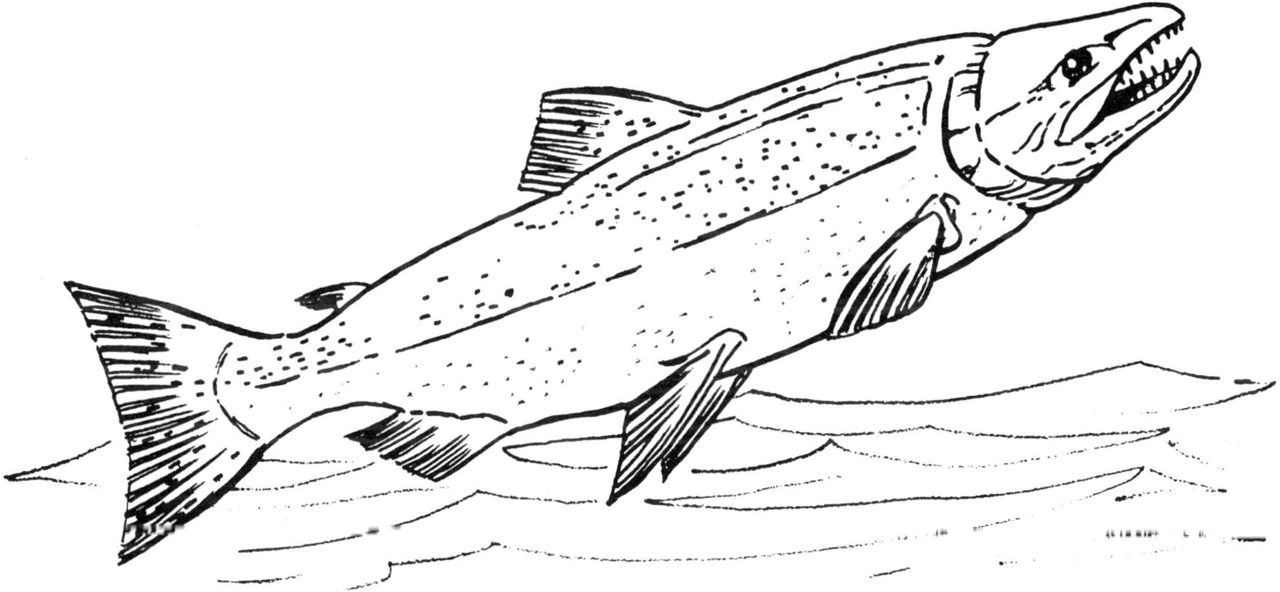

DUCK-BILLED PLATYPUS

Orinthorhynchus anatinus

The platypus has the distinction of being the least developed (most primitive) of all mammals. This 20 inch long 4 pound animal can only be found in lakes and streams of Australia and Tasmania. That bill you see is not hard, like a birds, but is soft and pliable, like leather.

••

The platypus' 1 to 3 eggs are incubated and hatched outside the mothers body.

DUCK-BILLED PLATYPUS

Orinthorhynchus anatinus

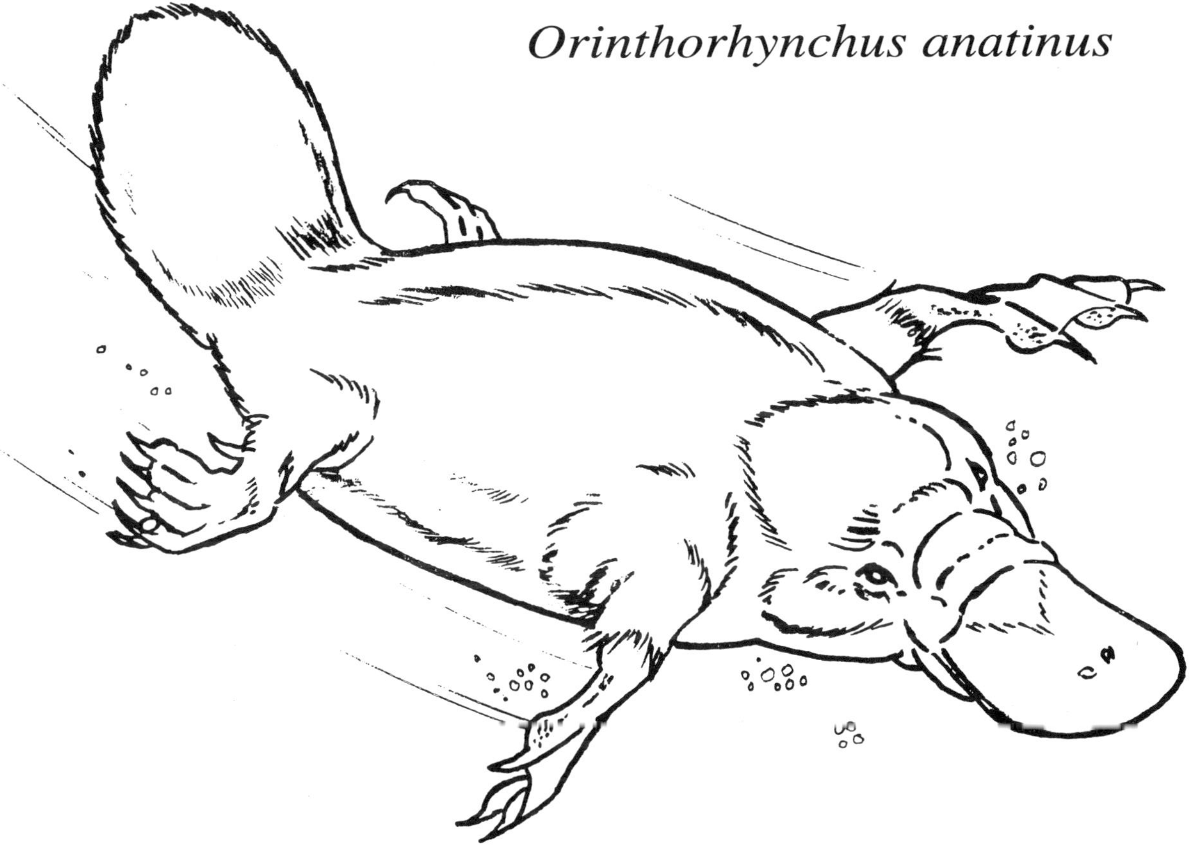

LEATHER BACK TURTLE

Dermochelys coriacea

This tropical (warm water) ocean turtle is huge. The worlds largest turtle can grow to be 7 feet long and weigh up to 1600 pounds. That is more than an average horse weighs! This powerful swimmer enjoys a tropical ocean home and is only found far from land.

The female lays several clutches of eggs that contain from 50 to 170 eggs each.

LEATHER BACK TURTLE

Dermochelys coriacea

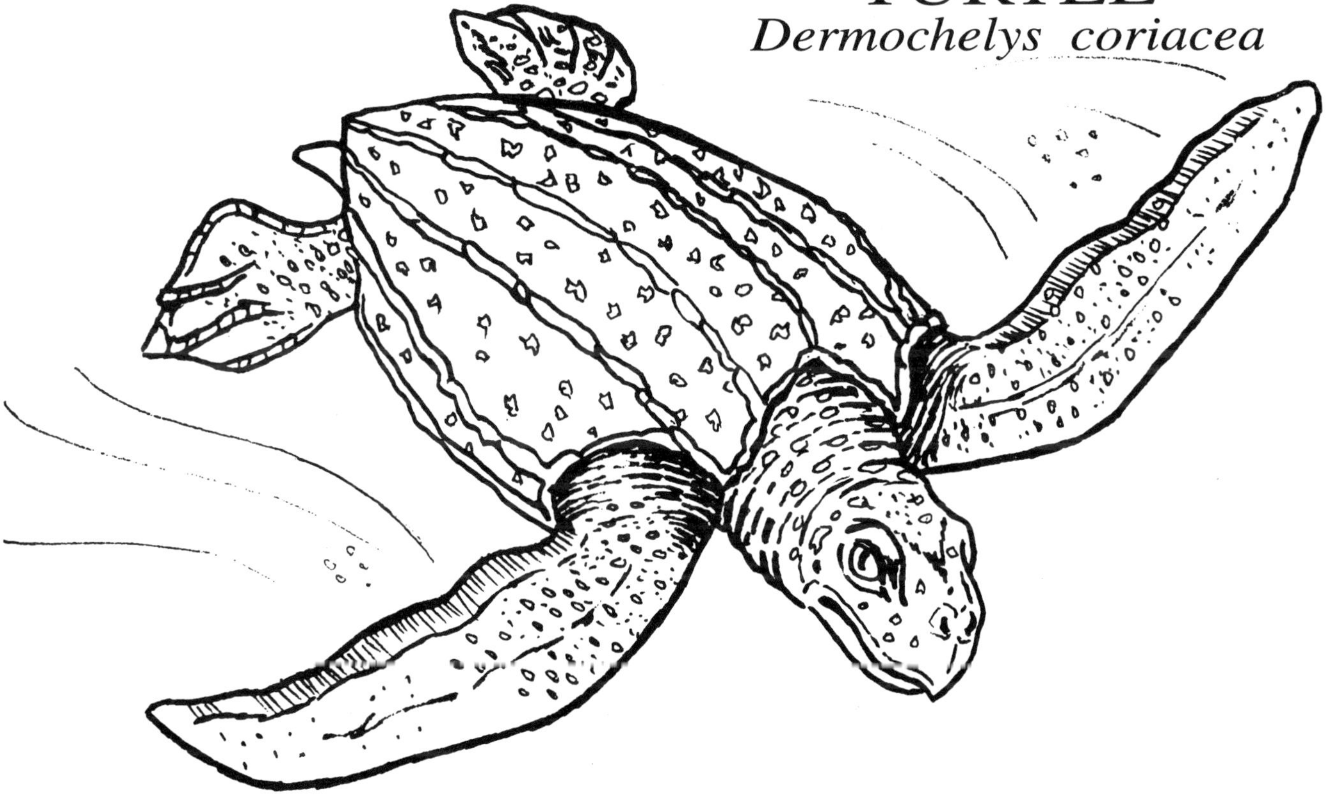

EMPEROR PENGUIN

Aptenodytes forsteri

The emperor is the largest penguin. They are the only ones to breed in winter. It is very cold, but they do survive. Winter breeding is strictly for the chick to be old enough to make its first trip to the ocean when food is most plentiful. The food can help insure future survival of the species.

The male places the single egg on his feet and covers it with belly skin to hatch.

EMPEROR PENGUIN

Aptenodytes forsteri

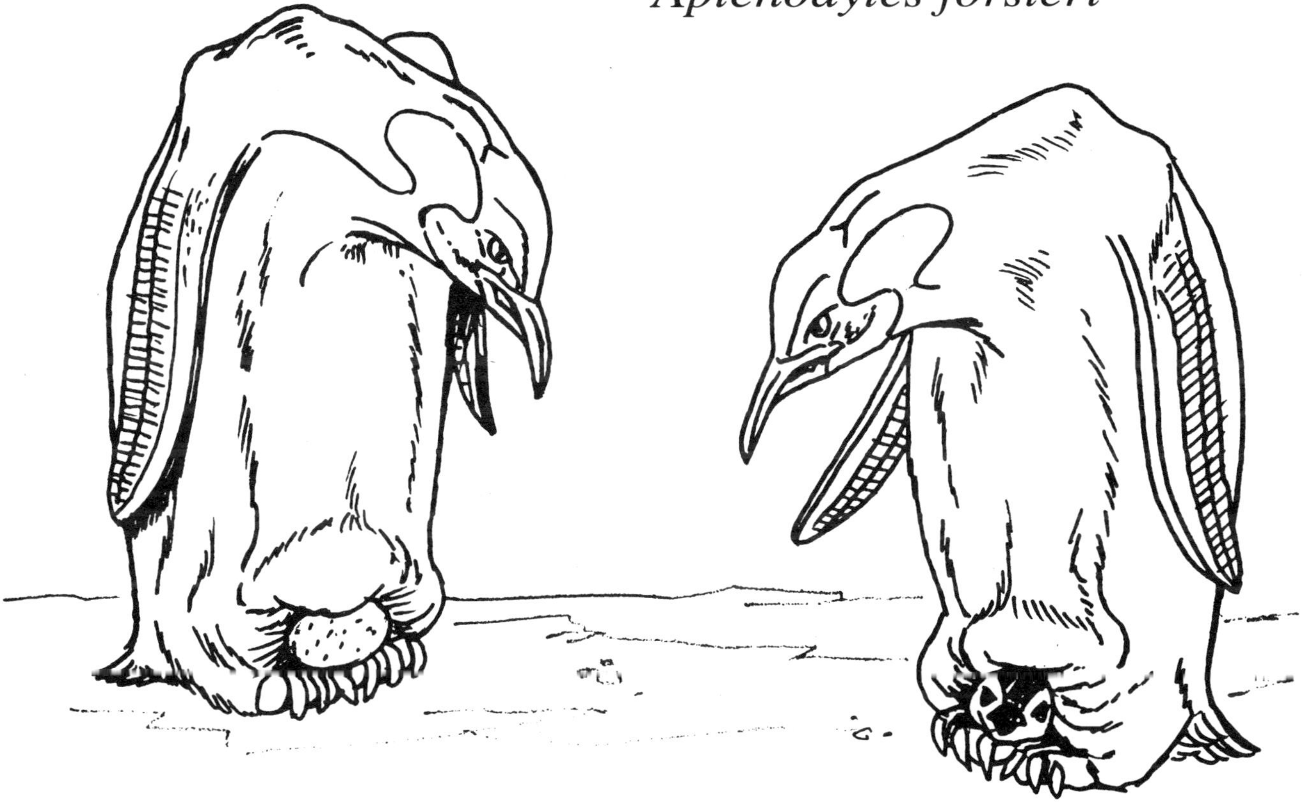

SWELL SHARK
Cephaloscyllium ventriosum

The swell shark prefers shallow waters of the Pacific Ocean, off the coasts of California and Mexico. At 4 feet, it is not a very large shark. When trying to scare someone away, or if it is frightened, it is able to draw air in and inflate itself to look twice as large as it actually is.

The female lays eggs each enclosed in a long pouch. Tendrils on the pouch anchor to coral until the embryo develops.

SWELL SHARK

Cephaloscyllium ventriosum

INDIGO SNAKE

Drymarchon corais

Georgia, Florida and Texas are home to North America's largest snake. The indigo snake can grow to 8 1/2 feet long, but is not poisonous. Besides a diet of frogs, small mammals and birds, the indigo snake can eat poisonous snakes without being harmed.

••

5 to 12 leathery shelled eggs are laid in April or May each year.

INDIGO SNAKE

Drymarchon corais

ECHIDNA OR SPINY ANTEATER

Tachyglossus aculeatus

This anteater is only 2 foot long and is commonly found throughout Australia and New Guinea. This primitive creature only eats ants and termites. Like the platypus, it is a member of the order Montremata (lowest form of mammals), but has some features of reptiles and birds.

••

A single egg is incubated, for 10 days, in a fold of skin on the mothers stomach.

SPINY ANTEATER

Tachyglossus aculeatus

CHICKEN

Gallus domesticus

The chicken has been a domestic animal for over 4 thousand years! For just as long, the crowing rooster has been the symbol of country living and rising with the dawn. Some species of chickens are bred for size, to weigh up to 12 pounds, while others are bred to produce eggs.

One chicken can lay 300 eggs a year.

CHICKEN

Gallus domesticus

AMERICAN ALLIGATOR
Alligator mississipensis

American alligators love the fresh water swamps of Florida, Mississippi and Louisiana. They probably like basking at the waters edge even more, now that they have been brought back from near extinction. We should be proud that we have passed laws to protect our animals.

•••

A 5 to 7 foot nest of mud and plants is filled with 24 to 60 hard shelled eggs.

AMERICAN ALLIGATOR

Alligator mississipensis

BALD EAGLE

Haliaeetus leucocephalus

This large bird is the national symbol of the United States of America. Eagles mate for life and continually add to their nest. Can you imagine a birds nest that is 7 feet wide and 10 feet deep? That is as big as a small bedroom!

••

Both parents incubate the 1 to 3 eggs in about 35 days.

BALD EAGLE

Haliaeetus leucocephalus

OTHER CHILDREN'S BOOKS CREATED BY SPIZZIRRI PUBLISHING

ISBN (INTERNATIONAL STANDARD BOOK NUMBER) PREFIX ON ALL SPIZZIRRI BOOKS IS: **0-86545-**

EDUCATIONAL READ AND COLOR BOOKS

ILLUSTRATIONS AND TEXT

SIZE: 8 1/2" X 11"

AIRCRAFT
ANIMAL ALPHABET
ANIMAL F. CALENDAR
ANIMAL GIANTS
ATLANTIC FISH
AUTOMOBILES
BIRDS
CALIFORNIA INDIANS
CALIFORNIA MISSIONS
CATS
CATS OF THE WILD
CAVE MAN
COLONIES
COMETS
Count/Color DINOSAURS
COWBOYS
DEEP-SEA FISH
DINOSAURS
DINOSAURS OF PREY
DOGS
DOGS OF THE WILD
DOLLS
DOLPHINS
EAGLES
ENDANGERED BIRDS
Endang'd Mam'ls-AFRICA
Endang'd Mam'ls- ASIA & CHINA
Endang'd Mam'ls-SO. AMERICA
ENDANGERED SPECIES
ESKIMOS
FARM ANIMALS
FISH
HORSES
KACHINA DOLLS
LAUTREC POSTERS
MAMMALS
MARINE MAMMALS
MARSUPIALS
NORTHEAST INDIANS
NORTHWEST INDIANS
PACIFIC FISH
PALEOZOIC LIFE
PENGUINS
PICTURE CROSSWORDS
PICTURE DICTIONARY
PIONEERS
PLAINS INDIANS
PLANETS
POISONOUS SNAKES
Prehist. BIRDS
Prehist. FISH
Prehist. MAMMALS
Prehist. SEA LIFE
PRIMATES
RAIN FOREST BIRDS
RAIN FOREST RIVER LIFE
RAIN FOREST TREE LIFE
REPTILES
ROCKETS
SATELLITES
SHARKS
SHIPS
SHUTTLE CRAFT
SOUTHEAST INDIANS
SOUTHWEST INDIANS
SPACE CRAFT
SPACE EXPLORERS
STATE BIRDS
STATE FLOWERS
TEXAS
TRANSPORTATION
TRUCKS
WHALES

SILHOUETTE ART BOOKS

8 1/2 x 11" Reproducible

CHRISTMAS
CIRCUS
DINOSAURS
FARM ANIMALS
OCEAN LIFE
ZOO ANIMALS

EDUCATIONAL ACTIVITY BOOKS

SIZE: 5 1/2 x 8 1/2"

Alphabet Dot-to-dot PETS
Alphabet Dot-to-dot ZOO ANIMALS
BIRD MAZES
BUTTERFLY MAZES
DINOSAUR MAZES
Dot-to-dot DINOSAURS
Dot-to-dot FISH
Dot-to-dot REPTILES
Dot-to-dot WHALES
FARM MAZES
FISH MAZES
FLOWER MAZES
MAMMAL MAZES
SHARK MAZES
SHELL MAZES
TREE MAZES
TURTLE MAZES
ZOO MAZES

EARLY LEARNING WORKBOOKS

SIZE: 8 1/2 x 11"

ALPHABET PICTURES
COMPLETE THE WORDS
COUNTING DINOSAURS
Dot to dot ALPHABET
Dot to dot NUMBERS
FIRST ADDITION
FIRST ALPHABET
FIRST NUMBERS
FIRST SUBTRACTION
MAKE A CALENDAR
MAKING WORDS
MAZE PUZZLES
NUMBERS and COLORS
PICTURE CROSSWORDS
PICTURE DICTIONARY
SHAPES, ART & COLORS
THEY GO TOGETHER
TRIANGLE PICTURES
WORD HUNT PUZZLES
WORDS IN WORDS

Educational FACTS and FUN Books

SIZE: 5 1/2 X 8 1/2"

ANIMAL LEAPS
ANIMAL SPEEDS
ANIMALS THAT LAY EGGS
ANIMALS WITH LONG NECKS
ANIMALS WITH LONG TAILS
BIRD SPEEDS
FOOTPRINTS OF BIRDS
INSECT HUNTERS
MAMMAL FOOTPRINTS
POISONOUS ANIMALS
SKATES AND RAYS
SMALL MAMMALS